MW01245864

FROM MY OWN PRISON TO REDEMPTION

HEALING FOR THE WOUNDED

by James S Horkey

DORRANCE
PUBLISHING CO
EST. 1920
PITTSBURGH, PENNSYLVANIA 15238

The contents of this work, including, but not limited to, the accuracy of events, people, and places depicted; opinions expressed; permission to use previously published materials included; and any advice given or actions advocated are solely the responsibility of the author, who assumes all liability for said work and indemnifies the publisher against any claims stemming from publication of the work.

All Rights Reserved
Copyright © 2022 by James S Horkey

No part of this book may be reproduced or transmitted, downloaded, distributed, reverse engineered, or stored in or introduced into any information storage and retrieval system, in any form or by any means, including photocopying and recording, whether electronic or mechanical, now known or hereinafter invented without permission in writing from the publisher.

Dorrance Publishing Co
585 Alpha Drive
Pittsburgh, PA 15238
Visit our website at *www.dorrancebookstore.com*

ISBN: 979-8-8860-4298-6
eISBN: 979-8-8860-4567-3

FROM MY OWN PRISON TO REDEMPTION

TO REDEMPTION

HEALING FOR THE WOUNDED

To a loving God, who stretched out His arm for me to grab just as I was about to drown.

To Karen, my wife, companion, and encourager.

And to Linda Alexander.

Thank you for believing in me.

CONTENTS

INTRODUCTION

After 54 years on this Earth, I was given direction from God to write a testimony and message of hope for those who never healed from being wounded. His words were, "Write the book. There is someone that needs to read it."

This book is a testimony based on a true story of an innocent child who suffered from the effects of trauma: what happened, what it was like, and what it is like now.

Trauma comes in many forms in the world today. There are wars where adults and children witness death by guns, bombs, and terrorist attacks. Others are survivors of rape, sexual assault, domestic violence, brutal assaults, kidnapping, torture, fires, plane crashes and auto accidents, just to name a few. If you are lucky, you may make it through life without ever personally knowing someone who has experienced trauma. If you do know someone, unless you are close to them, you most likely will only see the outside edges of the effects trauma and bondage has placed on them. That alone is enough to place you in a state of sorrow and compassion for what has happened to them.

You see, most trauma victims are masters of disguise. We can function in our daily lives, jobs, and get by in relationships and friendships making everything on the outside look good. I have learned that, for us, the pain we have is very deep within. In my case, parts were blocked out of memory, stuffed inside. A common thread among victims is self-destruction through negative thinking, depression, addictions, acting out, poor people skills, broken marriages, bad financial decisions, and a constant feeling of not wanting to be on this Earth any longer. I was able to juggle these characteristics all at the same time for decades. It was called survival.

I have often wondered how victims ever really heal to a point where they want to go on living and seek the purpose God has for them. After all, there is a host of specialized counselors, friends, pastors, self-help books, and countless other resources that could surely help the trauma victim. Why don't I hear more about success stories of healing, changed, and transformed lives? Part of the reason is, like me, most victims think they were at fault. We are ashamed of what happened, and after all, if we cannot even tell our parents, who can we tell? Living in this state, one can go on for years because we have adapted a form of survival. For me, it lasted almost 50 years before I had a recall of memory that was so horrific my only option was to live or die.

In my experience, healing had to come from God and through the resources and gifts He has blessed others with that could shift my thinking and heal.

My intention in creating *From My Own Prison to Redemption* was and still is to hope this book lands in the hands of the person who needs to read it.

As you travel through the book you will see how strong we as human beings really are, yet how weak we are when it comes to fixing things on our own. You must accept the gift of grace.

God can carry anyone through circumstances and difficulties in life no matter how terrible or how long they last, all to be used for His greater purpose.

PART ONE

WHAT HAPPENED

CHAPTER ONE

THE EARLY YEARS

I was born in November of 1960 in Michigan. On my birthdays, my parents would joke about how they barely made it to the hospital some 20 miles away due to a blizzard. These are the same people who told me they had to walk to school in knee-deep snow or ride on a horse drawn sleigh to school in the freezing temperatures. I cannot prove them wrong, but I am quite sure there were vehicles in their time as children, but to their defense, there may not have been school busses. Anyways, the story brought a laugh around the dinner table each year as I blew the candles out on my cake.

Well, I was second oldest in the mix of six children, all born about a year apart. I guess my parents being devout Catholics did not believe in birth control. For that, I am grateful because I am truly blessed to have had the parents I did and all my siblings.

I cannot say I remember too much of the first three years, but it was not long after that I still to this day can remember certain things, and my memory from age five on to this day, I can remember.

Kids play, and that is what we did as children. It was more like play and fight. You see, there were five boys and a girl. As a child, you do not even realize it, but you place an unbelievable level of trust in those around you. To think that there were no worries about what I was going to eat, what clothes there were to keep you warm, if there was a roof over my head. If you were sick, someone would ensure you were taken to the doctor; if you woke up at night from a nightmare, someone was there to hold you and rock you back to sleep. Everything was provided as best could be. Grant it, as a small child, you do not have the wisdom to even know you needed food, shelter, or clothing, so it seems like trust was easy. Looking back now and at our children and grandkids, it amazes me the level of trust they have, just like I did. Now in my wisdom, I struggle to trust my heavenly Father. A child makes it look easy.

The town I lived in had one stoplight, two grocery stores, nine bars, and the small hardware and department store, a Polish community of about 1,100 people, including the rural area. Growing up on a farm, there were always chores to do in addition to going to school. This type of living instilled a work ethic in me that shaped me for my future work life. Farming is not easy. I remember that it was a struggle financially as the price paid for crops and livestock changed daily just like the stock market.

My dad would try to balance the cost for seed, fuel, feed, livestock, equipment, and repairs along with providing shelter, clothing, and food for a family of eight on his small income from being a construction worker and farming after hours. With the climate in Michigan, you never knew if you were going to have a bumper crop or not. You may get a late start, getting seed into the fields due to a late winter or wet spring. There may be a drought in the summer and then a wet or early winter affecting the harvest season. The climate played a role in my father's employment as a construction worker. I remember, on a yearly basis, he would be without work for months. It just seemed tough to make a living with such a big family, but somehow my parents did it.

So life as a child goes on. When home, I had chores to feed the livestock, and as soon as I was old enough, I started to work in the fields. It is pretty country with rolling hills, woods, creeks, rivers, and lakes. The smells of the air in the spring, fall, and harvest season are something I will never forget. Growing up was about going to school and working after school on the farm. Of course, we had always made time to fish, trap, and go camping and exploring in the woods. Virtually everything we did was done as a family.

Growing up in the Catholic Church meant getting baptized within weeks of birth and attending church every Sunday and on holy days of obligation. Then you would get certain sacraments as you get older, some being the sacrament of communion, and sacraments of reconciliation and confirmation to name a few.

After kindergarten, I went to Catholic school. These were the days when they still had nuns teaching. I attended through seventh grade, and the parish had to drop the eighth grade due to lack of funding, so I went to public junior high for one year.

Everything so far sounds like a normal, structured upbringing for a child, but there are things interwoven in early childhood that would change me for years to come.

Chapter Two

The Trauma

From my earliest memory, I can still see and hear the screaming, yelling, and beatings that took place in our home. I was an adaptive learner but not immune to the discipline my father gave out when I did something wrong. Just as bad though was witnessing that discipline being done on my siblings. It may as well have been done on me because I could feel everything they did.

My mother did the best she could being a homemaker, trying to keep us kids under control, but all we needed to do was run outside when she needed something done or if she needed to correct us for something we did wrong. So her only choice was to report the daily events to my dad when he got home.

What that meant was whoever needed discipline that day got it with yelling and screaming so loud, your ears would hurt. Then the belt came off, and what seemed like non-stop whipping on the bare butt went on and on. Often there would be red strap marks left on the body.

I remember only getting a handful of this type of discipline because, as I said before, I was a quick learner. But my brothers got the brunt of it. There were times that I would curl up in the fetal position, hide behind the couch, and cover my ears when the screaming, yelling, and beatings took place. If you cried, there were more beatings until the crying stopped.

While hiding, my body would shudder as I heard the belt hit the body. My heart would seem broken, and when everything was done, there was an eerie quiet in the house. It reminded me of the quiet before the storm sensation. One would not dare go to the child who got it and console him or you'd risk getting beat yourself. It was every child for himself.

So by age six, I had already mastered the art of keeping guard, never wanting to disappoint my parents. It may have been the beginnings of my foundation around being a fearful, reserved, shy, and quiet child. Surely these would protect me going forward.

It took me years to believe that the discipline my parents inflicted on us in the 1960s was wrong. From what I gather, it was common to get slapped or spanked in public back then, even from a teacher. It was not only acceptable, but I believe it was a learned behavior my parents had based on how they were raised.

Looking at my own experience, I even started out with yelling at my children when they were young. I could never hit them though, but when I saw what the yelling was doing to them, I had to stop that too. I broke the cycle.

In today's world, there are surveillance cameras, child protective services, schoolteachers and counselors, doctors, nurses, psychologists, and law enforcement that all have a responsibility per their credentials to report abuse, even if it is heard but not witnessed.

So was it right or wrong? Times have changed, and back then spankings and verbal abuse were acceptable, but today it is not.

Recently, there was a sports figure who got turned into authorities for spanking his three-year-old child with a switch. Being a successful public figure, his career and financial income are in the balance pending the outcome of his hearing. When interviewed, he said he can see how what he did was wrong, but that is how he was raised.

Not defending his actions or my parents' way of discipline, but I do believe that these are learned behaviors. Unless we break the cycle, those of us who choose to discipline our children will suffer the consequences of children wounded for life, legal issues or both.

In my school years, I remember the kindergarten teacher holding my work in front of the class one day and telling everyone, "Now this is how not to do the work." I was embarrassed, and the kids laughed. I am sure it was not meant to be hurtful, but with my sensitivity already formed from my home life, it gave reason for me to now protect myself in my school life as well. I would do anything to keep from getting attention again.

So outside of the fact that I already did not like the way I looked and I was never particularly good in schoolyard sports, I kept to myself and focused on not getting called out for doing anything wrong.

Going to church as a child was like a ritual. When you are in the church, you are to behave and do everything that everyone else does. When it was time to stand, kneel, or sing, you did. You went to communion and frequently went to confession. It seemed like there were rules, and you could never be good enough. The church was full of tradition.

To me, the priest was the link between people and God. I perceived him to be a God figure himself because he preached, heard confession, burned incense, spoke in Latin, and dressed in holy robes. I really believed he could do no wrong. With my parents being devout Catholics, it was not uncommon for them to invite the parish priests over for dinner. They thought he could do no wrong either.

All I remember learning from the church is if you sin you go to hell. That alone made me fear the priest and most importantly fear God because I had already done so much wrong as early as four or five years old. I had no chance and was convinced I was going to hell. Yet I still did all the good Catholic stuff, attending church, confession, and every other tradition because I had to do what my parents said even though God hated me.

So by now, I was on guard against anyone with authority—my parents, teachers, priests, and God.

As a child, I was sexually molested between the ages of five and 11 by two neighbors, and at age eight I was molested and raped by the parish priest.

With the neighbors, it happened at many separate times individually. I remember being naked and watching him do things to himself and to me. After, he usually took a bath, and I had to watch that as well. Why I kept going over to that house, I may never know, but while there and if I was alone with him, the sex abuse was going to happen.

I just complied and looked like I was in a trance, in shock, with a blank look on my face. Each time I left, he said I was to say nothing or he would say I was lying. I really did not need that threat because the conditioning I already had from the discipline at home and my belief that God already hated me; there is no way I would have told anyone.

The other person who molested me was also molested by this neighbor. In his case, he ended up acting out from the sexual abuse that he endured. For me, I went further into myself, shutting down, lowering my self-worth, and feeling dirty. I did, however, start to seek the satisfaction of the feeling you get when you are intimate with someone. This was something I was taught in the abuse and something I could do to myself. I also started to identify with the big black hole inside my body, an empty feeling. I made an oath to never tell anyone, ever.

Nevertheless, I was able to blend in with my siblings and parents like nothing happened. I was already good at making thinks look okay on the outside.

At age eight, as an altar boy, I was preparing the mass sacraments of wine and bread for Holy Communion when the priest came around the corner and caught me sipping the wine and eating the bread. He scolded me, said I was a sinner and was going to hell. I was scared the most I ever had been in my life. To me, he was God, and that was as if God Himself was standing there telling me I was going to hell.

He then said he would not tell my parents if I would go through one-on-one altar boy training with him. To me, that was a great option because who knows what a beating I would have gotten from my parents?

The sexual abuse, which included rape, happened only three times. Each time, the priest would come into my class and ask the teacher for me. It was not uncommon for altar boys to have to leave class if there were a special Mass or funeral or something in order to help with the Mass.

In this case, there was no Mass, and there was no one-on-one training. Taking me into the rectory, we went into the study, where, after he dismissed the housekeeper for the day, he locked the door. There, he poured himself a glass of whisky and removed his pants and underwear. While he was sitting on a chair, he made me do things to him while he self-gratified himself. He would also play with me, and had raped me. It hurt so bad, I cried and bled. After, he would clean me up and get me ready to return to class. Each time, he said that if I ever told anyone, he would say I was lying because I was caught drinking wine and eating communion bread in the sacristy. A few years later, that priest was transferred to another parish.

After the third time, I had totally blocked this abuse out of memory. I was overloaded with trauma. I had full memory my whole life of the abuse by my two neighbors, but for some reason, I blocked this one out. It would evade my memory completely for another 40 years until I had a recall in April 2008.

Later in life, in the healing process, I had been asked why I was drinking at such an early age. After careful thought and in the process of getting to know myself, it was clear. You see, drink was prevalent in the town I grew up in. A one stoplight town with nine bars? I remember my grandfather and my dad going into town on Saturdays and hopping bars. For them, it was a time to socialize, drink, and play cards. As kids, we just played pool and waited for them to get done drinking, so we could go home. It seemed like every occasion in the community required hard liquor and beer. Be it a Polish wedding, a fish fry at church, first communion or confirmation party, or just a visit from friends, neighbors, or relatives. It was not unusual for people to have a second refrigerator just for beer or a keg of beer. Drink was also necessary if you worked in the fields and even at funerals for those who passed away.

Not knowing it at the time, I was experimenting with drink to fill an empty hole inside me. I was full of anxiety and fear over anyone with authority and surely did not want to upset my parents. I was already shutting down, holding in any outward emotion, and I did not act out from the various kinds of abuse I had experienced. I became an expert at acting like nothing was wrong. I look back and wish I had taken the risk to tell someone—anyone—what was going on even if they may not have believed me.

Making the decision on my own starting at age five to hold everything within set me up for an additional 40-year sentence in my own prison.

My biggest question I had for myself now approaching adolescence was, now what am I going to do?

CHAPTER THREE

THE VERDICT

Guilty on all counts and sentenced to life without parole, I came to realize that I had been in my own prison, and there was no release possible. It had been a year now that the sexual abuse had stopped. The harsh discipline from my dad was now focused on the younger children and us older ones were too smart to make him angry. At the age of 12, I had made the decision that I will do everything possible to protect myself from others harming me. I distinctly remember making this decision, and that sealed the foundation of my character I started to build years before, and this new way of living would get me through life going forward.

I remained reserved, quiet, and shy, traits I had already had for years. I had now added a new defense; I would be extremely cautious in every way, only letting others get to know me very little. I had also discovered how alcohol and marijuana could fill my emptiness, so I was able to go on.

My eighth-grade class was closed due to lack of funding, so I had to go to junior high for one year in the public school. That was a shock to me because I never had to switch classrooms or have different teachers for subjects. The class size was also larger than I was accustomed to, and I was new to the school. The other kids were already there for their sixth and seventh grade. They had friends; I had not and preferred it that way.

The situation did, however, make it possible for me to be teased a little. Kids made fun of my haircut, and my skills in sports were lacking, so I was always the last one to be picked to be on someone's team in physical education.

I remember we had to run around the track, and I heard kids laughing and pointing at me. The teacher told me to change my shirt because someone had spit on the back of my shirt. I was so embarrassed.

Having to shower after physical education was uncomfortable. I had already felt challenged sexually and did not like the way I looked, but I had to get in there with other kids anyway. Luckily, nobody made fun of me seeing me naked.

Other things that just freaked me out was that kids had girlfriends, holding hands and kissing. I often thought to myself, *Could I ever do that?* And quickly answered me, *No.* Not only was I so sexually damaged from the abuse, but I was so full of fear of every kind and felt much better by staying to myself. I was not going to break the promise I made to never let anyone hurt me or reject me again.

Kids were also skipping class, smoking across the road from school, and there were frequent fights. The fights I saw brought back the memories of earlier years and the discipline my dad gave us as defenseless young children. My throat would get sore, and my stomach would ache seeing a kid get the crap beat out of him. It felt as if it were happening to me.

So I managed another year. Following school, my home life was the same. I would go home to chores and working on the farm in the evenings. I really enjoyed that because it kept me busy and allowed for time to smoke weed and drink beer. In the 1960s and 1970s, it was the same as today's time. Even for a one stoplight town, whatever drug you needed was available, so having an older brother and cousins made it easy to get the dope and buy beer. Using drugs and drinking became a daily routine for me, and it felt great. I do not know how I hid it from my parents, other than I would work late into the evening and go downstairs to my room at night.

High school brought the same thing I had seen in junior high except there were more kids. Most kids had a large group of friends, and many of the boys had girlfriends. Right there, I was set apart. I could get by easier without having a girlfriend because I had such a low self-esteem sexually; I just wrote off that possibility. But friends, I needed to find some, and the best thing I had going for me is that I was experienced in dope and drinking. It did not take long to find a handful of friends who liked to do the same thing: smoke weed and drink beer or hard liquor.

I never applied myself to school as far as studying and was not good at math, but I did manage to get the credits I needed each year.

Getting to the age to get a driver's learner's permit gave me a chance to find more freedom. I bought my first car for $400. Between me and a couple of my brothers, I had 3,000 miles on that car before I even had my license. Working on the farm as a young child gave me the opportunity to gain experience how to drive tractors and my grandfather's truck, so all I really needed was the license.

I had gotten a job working after school in a tool and dye factory as a janitor, cleaning up the floors around the presses. This job gave me the money I needed for car insurance, clothes, and of course, my dope.

Having a car made it easier for me and my handful of friends to skip school. We would do this often in my sophomore and junior year. And all there was to do was cruise the country roads, drink, and do dope. By this time, I was now experiencing with all kinds of drugs. There was speed, mushrooms, acid, Qualudes, hashish, and the best weed I could find.

Keeping my few friends through my senior year was easy, as I became the supplier for drugs to them.

The one thing still lacking in my high school years was a girlfriend. I was okay with that because I was too shy to ask a girl to the dance or go to the drive in, and I certainly did not want to get rejected or hurt in any way. I remember always wanting one though because my older and younger brothers had no problem getting girlfriends. Sexually though, I could still achieve the feeling through my thought life with fantasies and acting out.

My friends never questioned why I did not have a girlfriend. Perhaps because they were too doped up and busy in their own lives to worry about mine, so pressure in this area was brought on by myself.

I remember having the courage to ask two girls out in those four years, and both dates turned into disaster. With one, I was so scared that I could not even sit next to her, hold her hand, or have a real conversation. She really wanted me to, but I did not. That was the first and last date with her.

The other gal, I had taken to the drive in, and I went out on a limb and started to hold her and kiss her. We began touching each other as well, but that is as far as I could get. I would pull back at that point because I felt so embarrassed and really did not know what to do if it went any further. There was no sex education in the schools, and my parents never did tell me anything about sex.

After a couple dates, I saw her riding around town with someone else. She never said anything to me again, and I felt rejected. How stupid could I be to let that opportunity go?

As minute as this seems, these two experiences set the stage for my relationships going forward.

I could now add rejection to the list of hurts, and that alone set the stage for me going forward in the few relationships that were to come. I graduated from high school with the minimum credits needed and was determined to stay in that town, work in the factory at night, and farm during the day like most everyone did.

The development of my thinking on my own was so engrained by now, it would shape the way I had dealt with all areas of my life going forward, especially in my work life and relationships.

What I thought would be helpful to me added to the dysfunction I had already endured. Sure, I had been hurt as a child by people who should love me, but now because of the way I dealt with that, I would place myself in a position to be hurt and do things that would self-destruct all areas of my life for the next 20-plus years.

I was incarcerated for life without parole in my own prison. Lucky for me, I had my own cell.

PART TWO

WHAT IT WAS LIKE

Chapter Four

Life Incarcerated

By now in my late teens, I had moved from a student into adulthood. The need to ensure protection for myself went to a new level. I was about to move out from my parents' house, and another layer of security was about to be gone. The only difference was that I now had to ensure I did everything possible to provide the shelter, food, clothing, and finances I needed for myself. The new level of responsibility shaped a belief system within me that said, "I am solely responsible for all my provisions, and I must do everything possible to ensure there is never gap in finances." Money was the primary source to all my needs. The pressure I put on myself to not fail in this area formed a belief system and determination within my core that would shape my work life for decades to come. Now, in addition to all I had been through, I had added a new role to my life.

As alone as I felt, the opportunity to flee the nest made it easier for me to go deeper within myself. Now it would be easier for nobody to know what is going on inside me.

Already being incarcerated for years, I began to accept the verdict and shaped my life around the fact that I would never be free.

I had recalled traits in my character back to early childhood and had accepted the fact that I would be this way the rest of my life.

Reflecting on my life, I reaffirmed the fact that I was guilty of placing myself in positions to be hurt sexually and emotionally. My identity was now formed that I would never have a meaningful relationship with a woman, and I could never trust anyone, ever.

Thoughts of suicide started to come frequently, and I felt at peace with the idea that I had already lived my life; there was nothing good in me or this world.

My profile, if you will, could be best described as a living in compartments. I could still identify as the little boy, the brother, son, student, adolescent, and now adult and sole provider completely responsible for every little detail in my life. I was always looking back or forward, rarely in the present.

Having these identities had seemed normal to me, but the pressure to maintain them all at the same time increased my fears and anxiety. My general outlook was always negative, and that is one area that was hard to hide from people.

The only way I could find temporary relief and escape from constant thoughts of failure and unworthiness were to drink and drug.

Having added the employee as a new identity, I was responsible to ensure I was successful. Thankfully, the work ethic I had learned growing up on a farm and helping my father on his side jobs in construction were and still are to this day a great asset. The downside in this identity was my perception that others should work as I do, and I had formed unrealistic expectations on myself, my peers and anyone with authority.

Employers love a person who will be on time and go beyond the expectations of the job. They work you until you drop.

I always thought that being an overachieving, diligent employee was the result of my work ethic, but years later I would find that although I did have an excellent work ethic, my drive, determination, and results were more the result of the fact that I had a little more control in this role as an employee than I did in my other identities. I was also driven by my need to not fail because now, not only would my family see me fail, but my employer and peers would form an opinion of me if I failed. This perception led me to believe everyone should work like I did. I found out that nobody approached their jobs as I did, and I felt resentment and anger to my peers for not pulling the load.

I started to have difficulties in my first full-time job with people in authority.

Growing up in Michigan, most jobs were in factories that supported the auto industry, and they were union jobs. I landed a full-time job on the graveyard shift in a plastics molding factory as a material handler. My job was to ensure the automated machinery never ran out of raw materials and to relieve personnel from their workstations at the machines for their break times. I was not a slave to a machine and had freedom to move about the factory and operate a forklift. I felt superior to the common worker, and I reckoned that my best work results were done while high. I really believed that because I would not have as much fear or low self-esteem while I was using and could therefore be more creative and take risks in decision making.

Drug tests, at that time, were unheard of in pre-employment screening, so it is no surprise that a high percentage of the people on my shift were on drugs, alcohol, or both during work hours. I seemed to attract to those kinds of people because we had something in common: We liked to get high. Within no time, I was using and drinking on the job like everyone else. At 7:00 A.M., after work, we would go to the bar and spend our evenings continuing the party.

I started to hang out with older people who never grew up. Sure, they had a house and a nice car, but the alcohol and drugs kept them back in time, like it stunted their growth in maturity.

It had been a couple of years since that horrible experience of having a date in high school, and I was fine without having a girlfriend. I had accepted that a while ago.

Then a woman at work started to befriend me. She was 15 years older than me, married, and had kids. She was a pot smoker, but no hard drugs or alcohol. I had found her spending time together with the people I did, so we would end up in the same car driving the country roads and partying after work. I vaguely remember the decision to take a risk in her interest in me was not a clever idea, but deep inside, I really was lonely and wanted a girlfriend.

So for months, I would end up spending time at her house. We would lay on her bed, talk, hold each other, and kiss, but that is as far as I would go. I have no doubt her intention was for sex, but there was no way I would go there. So, the friendship ended because I did not pursue her sexually. Inside, I was still clinging to be like other people, to have a relationship and have sex.

There was a big struggle within me to wanting a relationship and swearing off to never have a relationship. That type of thinking is like mixing water and oil. The side of never having a relationship gave me peace because I would not be able to be hurt that way. But the loneliness would soon place me in similar position again.

Being self-programmed to not want to get hurt in a relationship and not let anyone get to know the real me, coupled with my insecurity in my appearance and lack of experience in sex, it was no wonder this did not last long. Yet I felt like she rejected me.

I never thought of her husband and children being hurt if they found out that his wife, their mother, had interest in me, and I was at his house with her while he was at work and the kids were at school. Yet a few years prior, I got angry when the girl I had dated a few times in high school was dating another guy and was never to talk to me again.

So now, rejection by the opposite sex moved from being a fluke to a trend. I knew deep in my heart that females would hurt me and that was my destiny. Again, I swore off ever having another relationship.

Having a resentment spilled into my work life. I was now looking to get out, so I would not have to see her at work. I found a new job, and the grass was not greener on the other side, so I came back to my employer, and luckily, they brought me back.

The problem was, because they were union and had already replaced my position, I could come back but had to start at the bottom, working on the production line. I took the job, but reluctantly. Inside, I resented my employer. How dare they tell me to start over! I then started to make plans to get out completely, not only from the town but the state. Surely starting over somewhere else would be the remedy.

I decided to throw my clothes in my car and plenty of dope to hold me over until I found a new source and move to Arizona. I had a brother, uncle, and cousin who lived there, and I could get work painting homes, so I left.

I do not recall saying goodbye to anyone except my family. Outside of returning for my grandfather's funeral, I never returned to that town. It has been over 36 years now. Like other areas of my life, it was better to flee not fight. I remained in my own prison.

CHAPTER FIVE

INTERNAL BATTLES

With the geographical change, I was hoping for a do-over in life, but reality sunk in quickly that I was still in my own prison. There was no escape from me holding in everything that happened to me to this point. The verbal, physical, and emotional abuse of my parents; the sexual abuse; rejection from women; interpersonal difficulties with employers; and the belief that I was going to hell for all I had done wrong.

With those realities cleverly hidden in my character, I still had to make it appear on the outside that I was normal. To those around me, I thought I pulled it off, but years later, others always knew there was something about me they could not put their finger on.

I considered it success if I could just slightly fit in. If others would think that I was a nice guy, a little funny, that was all I needed. There was no way anyone would get to know the real me. That was so engrained by now, I did not even have to plan around that; it just became my normal operating mode.

I remained faithful to the Catholic Church, attending on Sundays, going to confession and holy days of obligation. Doing that did not take effort because that is all I knew my whole life. Going to church was just what you did; why, I had no idea. It was about rules and traditions. You went because you were told to your whole life. It was a habit and did not even occur to me to quit going because God hated me and I was going to hell anyway. Yet I attended church to fill the identity I had as a Catholic, to make outside appearances seem normal for my family. Back in those days, if you drifted away from the church, the family name would be marked by others in the church. There would be talk among the congregation: Is their child troubled? What is wrong with their family? And why are his parents allowing him to not attend church any longer? Is their faith in question? What kind of family is this?

Even though I was living away from home and a young adult, I still had the rule I made to myself when I was young. Whatever you do, never disappoint your parents.

Arriving in Arizona, my first order of business was to secure shelter. That was easy because my older brother had moved there, so I was able to stay with him until I found something more permanent. Second, I needed to find a new source for my drugs. This was a little more of a challenge because now I was no longer the supplier but back to being the common user. Thankfully, drug users are easily found; it is like we attract to each other, and I was able to locate a steady source before I ran out of my stash. Drinking and drugging were a daily ritual. There was nothing in this area that gave me the idea that I might be in an addiction, even though by this time, I had been using daily for almost nine years. There were no consequences: I was able to keep a job; there were no legal problems; it was fun; and most of all, it was what made me feel normal, and I could fit in.

Settled in, I could now embark on a new life far away from where I grew up. The one thing I could not get away from was the internal struggles. Nothing within me changed in this geographical move. I was still a prisoner with different identities and compartments to manage. So I was there in a new place but needing to maintain my reality. This took extreme energy and management on my part to hide the real me.

The next 12 years would bring about more relationships, infidelity, and hurts that I just added to the pile of rubbish within me.

Because I tried to play the role of a normal person, the need to have a girl-friend was critical even though I had already predicted to myself it would be a disaster. I mustered up the courage to ask this gal out, and we became friends. She was easy to find because I only hung around dope users. So we started to see each other daily, and one time, we had sex. I cannot believe I did it with no experience or instructions; it just happened. I had no clue to consider protection from STDs or getting her pregnant. I knew nothing about that. Thankfully, nothing in those areas happened.

It was only a couple of months when I noticed she was hanging around another family in the apartment complex, and one of the family members was a male was about our age. I would see them together around the pool, and eventually she stopped coming over to see me or would say she was busy when I wanted to see her.

It was right then I knew she was with him. Again, I had been rejected, thrown to the side. I had asked myself again, *What is it about me that women end up dumping me?* The pain inside me was worse than the anger because I could easily blame myself for her actions. I would heap piles of evidence on me that said I was not attractive, I was too shy and quiet, I was not a touchy-feely guy, and now I could add that I was no good at sex. My general attitude now was that life sucks and then you die.

There would be nothing that could convince me that I was not the problem; after all, every so-called relationship I had been in ended this way. Thanks to alcohol and dope, I was able to mask the pain and hurt and make this problem go away; at least temporarily.

Every single time I became hurt or disappointed, I would end up in a tailspin, reliving my past clear back to a little child. I could still see myself and my siblings being beat and yelled at, the sexual abuse, being made fun of at school, desperately seeking friends but never letting anyone get close. It is like my life always went back as it was moving forward. Managing all this at one time was exhaustive, but to me, it was normal. It did not appear to me that normal people do not struggle with the past. It was because most people have a family member or close friend they can talk to about anything, and that helps them through tough times.

My whole life was buried within me, the good and the bad. I never opened up to anyone about anything, so I had no idea that was even an option, and if it were, I had already told myself I would never share my past. I was not only embarrassed, but I was to blame for everything that ever happened to me.

Having a relationship with a female was, to me, a requirement that showed outwardly that you were complete. If my parents, family, and friends saw that I was a loner and had little interest in women, well…that would lead to questions. I am not sure when I first believed that having a woman in my life was a requirement, but I am certain it was after the sexual abuse, and seeing my brothers having girlfriends meant I had to keep up.

So I continued to strive for this identity to make myself as complete as possible. Knowing in my heart that another relationship would be a disaster, I had no choice but to get into another one. I would not allow people to think something was wrong with me.

In general, on the outside, I was able to function. Months after I moved, I had landed a job at a fortune 500 company. So the role of my work life was secured. One could say I did not want to work and better myself, but my career there would last almost 17 years, and I would have much success learning various jobs in distribution logistics, receiving accolades and getting promotions.

Fortunately for me, this was a key identity I was able to manage due to my strong work ethic, the downside being that I was extremely critical of myself and my performance. I was never satisfied with my results and never really enjoyed the success I really had. As much as I did not want this to show, others noticed my negativity against myself. Physically, it would show in my face, and outwardly, I would say things that others would interpret as having a low self-esteem or never seeing anything good in myself, yet my managers saw my results, and I would move up in the company.

I was at a party and happened upon three girls who needed a roommate. I had no idea where the courage came from given my history, but I accepted. We all lived and partied together for about a year, and then I got my own apartment, taking with me the gal who showed the most interest in me. Finally, again it would look normal for those looking in from the outside.

This relationship lasted only a few years. There were good times; we had similar interests, and she liked to smoke pot. One thing we had in common was the lack of experience in sex. She was a virgin, and at that time, I had only had sex two times. The stress of having sex was not a big deal at first, but as time went on, I convinced myself that I was the one who would make her happy. Boy, was I in for a surprise! In the years that we were together, I never succeeded because I was too nervous, had no self-confidence, and was hurt by previous relationships. The pressure was too much, and I started to put myself down for not being able to achieve intimacy. My drinking increased, and my dope use continued as well. I would drag her into my negativity, and I am sure that did not help as well.

One New Year's Eve, we were at a party, and about 2:00 A.M., I was looking for her and went into the other room and saw her with another man. Her top

FROM MY OWN PRISON TO REDEMPTION

off, and they were making out. They saw me and stopped, I turned around without saying anything and left the party.

That same hurt from previous infidelity came back and was magnified because now she sought out the intimacy she could not have with me because I could not please her.

The next day, I was angry and would not forgive her for what she did. I remained drunk for days and doped up. I would say ugly and hurtful things, but I would not tell her I was a worthless piece of crap incapable of being a man who could provide intimacy. I had convinced myself she was justified in what had happened, but I would never tell her my secret.

It was about this time that cocaine was now part of my solution. I had recently stopped hard liquor because I did not like the effect of a hangover. Beer was my beverage of choice; pot, acid, mushrooms, and cocaine were my comfort as well. I had always heard that cocaine would take you down, but I managed to use and still pay my bills, so to me, I did not have a problem.

Towards the end of this relationship, I felt the need for revenge, so I was skiing in northern Arizona one weekend and had a one-night stand with someone I met at the ski lodge. I was much surprised at the outcome. It was the only time in my life I felt like I performed and felt she was pleased. I justified to myself it was because we did not know each other and would never see each other again. I was also extremely drunk and high on my newfound friend, cocaine.

The relationship ended a few months after that. She never found out about my infidelity, and for some reason, I did not feel like I did anything wrong. You would think that after everything I had been through and the hurts brought on to me by other women, how it is I could do what was done to me? Even worse after it was done, I refused to believe I did anything wrong and did not think of the level of hurt I would have put on her if she found out. No, it was still all about me.

It was during this relationship that my parents and the rest of the kids moved from Michigan to Arizona. The climate was a big motivator. There were good times, such as family playing cards on weekends, family get-togethers, and so on. They really liked this gal, and now I was under pressure to replace her, so they would not think something was wrong with me.

So here I go again, reliving and regretting the past. Putting blame on myself and reaffirming my inadequacies. The depression was much deeper now;

suicidal thoughts were common, and I was hoping for an accident to take me out. I was ready to go. I hated my life, and I hated myself.

Coming to the realization that I was still on this Earth, I needed to fill the void. I had met this gal at work, and we had started to date. It was not long that we had moved into a place together. Again, I was able to put together a few years in a relationship. She felt comfortable sharing with me her childhood hurts and disappointments, which had similarity to mine, but I could never let her know I had been abused as well.

In this timeframe, I had stopped using the psychedelic drugs and settled for alcohol and pot. She was a pot smoker but not much of a drinker, perhaps because she was an adult child of an alcoholic father. I did not know for years the affect I had on her from my drinking. Her parents were also divorced, and that was my first experience even knowing anyone who came from a broken household.

After four years of living together, I asked her to marry me. She said no, and I was hit with a ton of bricks. I did not ask her why, and she did not offer. I, of course, blamed myself for not being the man she needed, but it was more about how she felt about herself and the relationship blunders she had in her past. I wanted to kill myself on the spot—*what a failure I am!*—but we managed to still live together, and I proposed again about a year later. This time, she said yes.

I started to notice her hanging around this married guy at work, and one night, she did not come home. When I asked her about that, she admitted she was with him. I lost it, and my anger and rage was taken out on her with yelling and screaming. Feelings that I was the problem again were beyond manageable, and although I knew I was the problem, outwardly, I made sure she knew she was the problem.

With the family knowing of our plans to marry, I could not leave her; what would they think? I also could not tell anyone of her infidelity; what would they think of me? So I had to go forward, knowing in the back of my mind this was not too bright of an idea. I mean, if she had already cheated on me, what would happen when we are married?

Some time went by, and the factory was shutting its doors. I managed to get a job with the same company in El Paso Texas, so we moved to New Mexico. This geographical change would be good for us. At least she would not be near that guy.

I was not smoking as much dope now, but I was drinking like a fish; still needing to fill the big black hole in my gut.

Success in my job earned me the opportunity to travel on business several times per year. We had started to plan our wedding and got married back in Arizona about a year later. Within seven months of marriage, I came home from a business trip to find my wife crying on the couch. After prodding her for what was wrong, she confessed that she had an affair, got pregnant, and was sick from an abortion gone badly.

All I remember was a reaction of zero tolerance. I was so numb that depression and suicidal thoughts were put on hold. I am sure I was angry at her but was more concerned about damage control. How would I explain this to my family? Surely we would divorce, and that was unheard of in a Catholic family.

Ensuring she got the right medical attention, I calmly arranged for her to move out of the house I had just bought less than a year before. I filed for divorce, taking all the bills, sold the house, did a voluntary repossession of a vehicle, and filed my first bankruptcy. I moved from New Mexico to El Paso. There was nothing left for me there.

Then the depression hit; anger at myself; and now I was praying for death in any way. Not living in Arizona any longer made it easier for me to hide that fact that I was no longer married, but I could only pull that off for about four months.

As much as I did not want to disappoint my parents, I had to tell them over the phone that I was divorced. To my surprise, they did not judge me, but I could never forgive myself. I was the one to blame. I knew that I was inadequate sexually, drank, and was full of negativity. Surely, I was the one who drove her to this. It would be 11 years later before I would talk to her and forgive her for what happened, but most importantly admit my wrongs and ask for forgiveness.

I went about a year focused on my career, but the reality of being alone won out again. I needed to bring someone into my life again. Even though I drank daily, I was never into going to bars or night clubs. I could not dance, and I did not have the courage to ask anyone to dance. So for me, to go to a club meant to sit in a corner and not talk to anyone all night, then go home at last call.

It did not even occur to me that at almost 30 years old, I did not even have any male friends I could spend time together with in the evenings and weekends. I never did have friends, so that did not seem odd to me, but in looking back, that was just a way for me to keep others from knowing me and made hiding my past easier.

One night, I said to myself that I would never meet anyone staying home, so I had better get out. I went to a country and western bar, and after a few drinks, a gal asked me to dance. We had dated after that and a couple of years later got married. Our first child was born nine months later.

Even though I still drank daily, I did cut way back on smoking pot. Maybe because I was getting older, it seemed like it did not take as much for me to get high, and it was harder to be in public while high. My wife did not use drugs and rarely drank.

The same year we were married, I had transferred with my work to Austin, Texas, where we had our first child. I had also met up with a couple people I used to work with in Arizona who were now in Austin. That brought the opportunity to rekindle old-time memories, and in no time, I was doing cocaine again with them.

In 1993, we had our second child; I was promoted into management, and we had built our second home. Everything on the outside looked good.

Then I had a clear revelation that my cocaine use was of concern to me. I was doing strange things to get cocaine, and I was starting to use it daily. Nobody on the outside told me because nobody knew how much I was using, and up to that point, I hid it from my wife. I found myself taking cash advances on my credit cards to buy cocaine with the solemn vow to pay the card off with my next check. That, of course, never happened. The warning to myself that I might have a problem was not enough for me to do anything about it. To my surprise, I would end up going an additional seven years using cocaine daily and racking up debt until I could not get any more credit.

I had a major surgery about two months after my promotion into management, and our second child was only one month old when I got a phone call that my mother unexpectedly died from a stroke. I got the call the same night our child was being baptized in the Catholic Church.

I just could not manage anything good or bad at that point, and I started using more cocaine. At my mother's funeral, I was so jacked up, I could not even cry. I felt bad I never even sent her a picture of our son and that she had not met him. Even though she never understood the extent of my obvious addiction or anything I had gone through my whole life, she never got to see me draw a sober breath.

I do not know if I used her passing as a reason to dive deeper into my cocaine use or if it was the natural progression on a disease, but it happened. Financial difficulty reared its ugly head, and now my wife was on to me. Not only was I acting strangely, the family unit was falling apart. My physical appearance had an ashy look to my skin from using so much cocaine, I was sick.

My work life suffered in the fact that I started to use cocaine during working hours. My management position made it possible to heap unrealistic expectations on my employees, and I soon started to have difficulties again in my work life.

With my wife on me hard for a couple of years, I entered my first outpatient rehab. I was looked up to by the group because I grasped the concepts of recovery and made it look like I was doing the deal. In the last week of the rehab, I was kicked out for a dirty drug test. Now I could add failure in rehab to my resume.

Chapter Six

The Spiral

As is common with most drug addicts and alcoholics, we do not see the severity of our problem until it is way past the point of being able to do something about it on our own.

Using drugs and alcohol for about 23 years to this point, I recalled knowing inside that something was wrong for the last three years but could only wish the problem would go away. I tried everything in my power and had a sincere desire to stop destroying myself, my family, and my finances, but nothing was sufficient to stop the progression of the disease.

It seemed that the harder I tried or wished, the worse it got. I had already been going to Twelve Step meetings for years to show my wife I wanted to stop, but it never clicked. I could not identify with those in the meeting, and I just showed up, never opening the book or getting a sponsor, but I continued to go.

My life was falling apart. In the past, I would have been hung up over my appearance, my low self-esteem, my inability to please a woman sexually. I just accepted those as part of my makeup, and now my biggest problem was that I was a loser hooked on drugs and alcohol yet able to keep a job, shelter, food, and clothing for my family, but barely hanging on.

Addiction is a vicious spiral when in the final stages. I would admit to myself I was insane, and I had believed that God wanted me to die as an addict. That was my punishment for my sin so many years ago.

Still thinking God hated me, I did attend church regularly like any good Catholic. Why, I do not know, but again I did have the opportunity to hide my addiction from my father and my siblings, and I mostly used by myself. I did not frequent clubs or hang out with other addicts, so keeping a job, a family, and attending church would appear from the outside that everything was okay. It was okay for me and my wife to know I had a problem but my energy focused on how to keep my employer, my extended family, and our few friends from knowing anything.

As time went on, things got worse. For me to be able to use the drugs, I needed money, and my income, although sufficient, was not enough to pay the bills and provide the cash necessary for my habit. It was not long before my wife had to take a second job to help pay the bills. I was taking out pay day loans, borrowing from loan sharks, stealing from family and my employer, and pawning everything could. This continued through the end of my using career, which was still years off.

It is amazing how the mind can trick you into believing that this will be the last time, only to find out that the next day I was doing the same thing again.

Fearing that my employer was noticing my quirky personality and my paranoia, that they would soon put two and two together and confront me with their suspicions that I might have a drug or alcohol problem, they never got a chance to confront me because I made plans to leave the business. I had a restructuring exercise at work to take an early retirement, and I jumped on it. This ended an almost 17-year career with a great company, all so they would not know I had a problem.

I landed another job, and my father was then diagnosed with terminal cancer. Things were really getting out of control with my addiction, the family, and the stress, so I had seized the opportunity of having a terminally ill father and told my employer I needed to leave the state for 30 days to be with him.

I never went to see him, and instead I checked into a 30-day inpatient facility. That way, my employer would not have to know. My prior treatment was outpatient, so I managed to hide that from my employer as well. I spent more time making things look like there was not a problem than addressing the problem.

I got through that treatment clean and sober, felt great, rested, ate healthy food, and gained knowledge. What I lacked in that treatment center was a first step experience, so all I really got was time away from work, drugs, alcohol, and family. It would not be but two weeks after leaving treatment that I was right back to where I left off, using so much, I had to start stealing and pawning again just to get by.

Inside, I felt doomed, failing again at treatment. The disappointment on my wife and the burden she bore to keep things going showed on her as well. I began to believe I was a failure at treatment and started to accept that I would die an addict.

I really did want to stop but held on to my belief that I had to do something to stop. What I had learned years later was there was absolutely nothing I or anybody else could do to end my addiction. I was beyond human aid.

I had been blessed with another job, so I had justified that if I was able to keep a job and a family, I must not be as bad as those people in the meetings. They had told stories of multiple DWIs, possession charges, foreclosures, broken marriages, wrecked vehicles, on and on. That was not me, yet why was my life so bad? I knew I could not stop because I had tried. I could not put sober days together let alone weeks.

I can remember birthdays, anniversaries, and Christmastimes where I left the house with money in my pocket, headed for the store to buy gifts, and with every fiber in my being having the intention to get those gifts. Suddenly while on the way, an overpowering thought to score cocaine and drink became paramount, and I never, ever made it to those stores. I had fought those thoughts, even crying all the way to the dope dealer's house, but my addiction won out every time. Again, I would have to face my own guilt and shame and see the despair on my wife's face when I got home.

My father died that same year, and all the sudden, the pressure to have to hide my addiction from my family was relieved. My siblings did not know the severity of my addiction because we did not live in the same state, and to me, if they found out, so what?

So nothing changed. I still had to use on a daily basis. I went to work and went to Twelve Step meetings, then I would have to go home and feel the shame of what I was putting my family through.

My wife ended up having me served with divorce papers and asked that we separate, so she could protect herself and the children. Having to move out of the house, I could now add to my list of failures the fact that I was a lousy husband and father.

All this new problem did was give me more reason to drink and drug. My credit was good enough for me to qualify for a small apartment, but that was short lived, as my finances could not keep up with the bills. I ended up getting out of one lease and into another right before things went south and eventually ended up getting evicted.

With nothing left to cling to, the only identity that was still intact was my work life. I was able to keep a job but not a place to live. How crazy is that?

Words cannot describe the loneliness, despair, and insanity of being slave to addiction. I had prayed for God to just take me. It did not matter if it was from a car accident, murder, suicide, overdose, or a natural death. I just wanted out, and I wanted out now.

It amazes me how addicts are so resourceful in their planning and being able to juggle so many problems at once. We are a resourceful, determined lot and will find a way if there is one to get done what we need.

Who else could, being homeless, manage to keep a job, look clean, still have transportation, and yet make sure there is enough money to keep the habit going? And make it look to others that nothing was wrong. I am sure others knew something was very wrong, but in active addiction, we do not see what they do.

Chapter Seven

I Wish It Would End

With almost nothing left, I was faced with the truth as I saw it. I had to accept that I was still incarcerated with no hope of release.

By now, I had already been separated from my wife and kids over two years and I was homeless. The only thing I had left was my job and my drive to support my two small children, who had nothing to do with my problems.

Even in the deep addiction, I was able to perform at my work, and I would make sure I sent child support even though the court had not yet mandated that I do. My addiction also required I have income to keep it going, so I still had to steal, pawn, and do whatever was necessary to cover that need as well.

Stuck in a deep depression, I now accepted that I was a lousy husband, poor provider for my kids, a homeless bum, drug addict and alcoholic, responsible for two broken marriages, repossessed vehicles, bankruptcies, a failure at treatment, a loner, responsible for the hurts women and men had placed on my life and convinced I was going to hell. It was just a matter of time before my employer caught on and would fire me. The only good thing in me was I honestly had the desire and did provide for my children financially.

I was living in my vehicle north of Round Rock, Texas, at a public rest area. The advantage being that the law cannot harass you there because those are intended to be a place of rest for travelers. I never arrived much before 9:00 P.M. in the evening and left for work by 7:00 A.M., so I fit in well.

I was able to wash up, shave, wash my hair and brush my teeth at the rest stop, so in general, it did not appear to anyone at work that I was homeless.

Being insane, I would justify in my mind that being homeless was not that bad. After all, there was no mail delivery with delinquent bills, no rent to pay, no water or electric bill. Even though it was wintertime, the climate in Texas made it bearable to sleep in a vehicle and not freeze to death.

I went on about my daily routine which by now only consisted of going to work, making my car payment, drinking, and drugging after work, and driving to the rest stop to sleep at night.

I had to spend every ounce of energy to just do these things because the addiction still had hold of me. Everything revolved around how I could get enough money to pay child support, make my car payment, keep my employer from finding out I was an addict and homeless, and getting my daily fix of cocaine and alcohol.

I was not able to make ends meet, so I finally had to quit making car payments, and it was not long before the repo man showed up. This time at my workplace and in front of everyone I had to go into the lobby and sign off on him towing the vehicle. Every possession I had was in that car, which only consisted of clothing and a few material things. That was a new low for me because, before now, I was able to hide my difficulties from everyone. I could do damage control but not in this case.

Nobody at work ever said anything to me about the wrecker taking my car. That was nice, but I am sure people had seen that and were talking.

Now I needed shelter. What was I to do? It was pay day, and I had known a guy at work who just bought a new car. I asked him if he would sell his old vehicle to me, and he did. It was an old Suzuki Samurai, two-seater. I did the right thing in my mind and used that paycheck to buy the vehicle instead of buying drugs that day.

I drove to the pound and got the few possessions out of my vehicle. I remember thinking I was back to normal.

My mind at this point was really racing with constant thoughts of suicide, thoughts of death and just not wanting to be on this earth any longer. I had already been on anti-depressants and Antabuse. I had seen counselors, psychologists, and doctors and had been through two rehabs by now, but nothing worked. I would never tell anyone about my problems, not even my siblings, but for some reason, I was honest with my doctors. I figured I had nothing to lose with them because by law they cannot tell anyone anyway.

It was Christmas week 1999, and out of fear that I might take my own life, I had check in to another outpatient rehab. This time, it was a place that had a bed for homeless patients. What a deal. I had heat, a bathroom, shower, and I could still leave in the morning for work, and nobody would know what was going on, again.

The facility really wanted to help me, but I was not ready. Yes, I could say to myself that I was out of control and did not want the disease, but that is as far as I got. I just was not through yet. Not even a gift of warm shelter in a hospital could keep me from using. Right before New Year's Day, I was discharged for a dirty drug test.

The little glimmer of hope that I had was gone. Snuffed out for good. It was back to the living on the side of the highway. My life unchanged, I really started to get depressed, and I spent every waking hour thinking about suicide or wishing for a tanker truck to cut me off on the highway—anything to leave this Earth.

I attempted to overdose a few times, but I guess God would not allow it. I was so mad at Him. *Why won't He let me go?* I was convinced that God had this plan for me; I prayed that He would take me. I was ready to go.

Down to three things left, which were to go to work, providing financially for my kids, and drinking and drugging, I went on. My life was miserable, and I spent nights crying myself to sleep, curled up in the fetal position of that small vehicle at the rest stop, praying and hoping I would not wake up in the morning.

The sun would rise again. Even without a car payment, now the progression of the disease still required even more drugs and alcohol. I continued to steal from my employer and pawn anything I could. By now, my family was tired of me manipulating them out of money that would not get paid back, and my options were quickly dwindling. Even the drug dealers quit fronting me my supply because I could not pay on time. So now the only thoughts racing through my mind were, *How do I not wake up in the morning?* and *How do I get dope?*

I already started to do drive offs at gas stations for fuel and would walk out on restaurants after eating huge meals and drinking. Every dime I made now went to child support and drugs, nothing else.

The walls in the jail cell were closing in on me, and I started to plan a suicide. In rural Texas, there are farm-to-market roads, and I found a narrow stretch of road out in the middle of corn fields that had a hair pin curve with no sign indicating there was a curve. It was a road only traveled by the few farmers in the area, but the best part was a tree in the ditch of the curve. This tree was an old oak as wide as my vehicle. My plan was to hit the tree head on at a high rate of speed with no seat belt on, convinced that the impact would kill me instantly.

I drove the area and paced it out several times, then set a date to do it. My plan was to have no drugs in my system, and on a foggy morning, I would drive out there and, at a high rate of speed, drive straight into the tree. It would look like an accident, and I would be clean at the time, so the investigation would agree it was a tragic accident. I was so desperate to die, I was able to stay clean for the 30 days I needed for weed to get out of my system.

I could not sleep the night before I was going to end my life. Dawn came, and sure enough it was a very foggy day. I drove out to the road where I would end my life, crying out to God why He wanted me to do that. Suddenly, a moment of clarity hit me. Even though in my planning process I had justified to myself that this would look like a tragic accident, something came to my mind at that point that said:

"Wait. You may fool people, but eventually your kids will find out that you struggled with drugs, alcohol, depression, and abuse and decided to take your own life." It hit me that if my kids thought that Dad found a way out from his demons, then it would be okay for them to do the same thing if they were ever to experience difficulties.

The thought that I could be responsible for an action they may take later in their life stopped me from going through with my own suicide.

Now I felt even more hopeless because I could not even take myself out. I was out of options, so it was back to drugs and alcohol.

I have had low spots in my life, ever since I was a small child, I wanted to die. Those thoughts seemed normal to me, but this low spot really hit me.

Still working, I had health insurance, so I had made an appointment with my primary care physician. I had been honest with him in the past, and he did everything he could to help me with medication, referrals to psychologists, and entry into rehabs.

I explained my deep depression and my inability to quit drinking and drugging again, but this time stopped short of telling him about my attempted suicide. He knew I always had thoughts, but if he knew I had a plan and started action on that plan, by law, he could have had to report me and send me straight into a psych ward.

In my mind, if that happened, my employer would then find out about my addiction and mental illness, and I would lose my job.

I could not lose my job because that was all I had left, and I need to support my children financially because they did not do anything to deserve a deadbeat dad.

The doctor promised that he would see what he could do to get me into inpatient rehab. He asked if I would be willing to go understanding that my employer would need to know, and he explained that addiction was not uncommon; that employers deal with this all the time.

I said I would go if he could make it happen. My life went on with not much to cling to other than going to work, drinking and drugging, and living on the side of the highway. It had been over a year now that I had cut off all communication with my family. The only interaction was with my kids on the weekends.

The divorce was finalized as well. I never got an attorney or contested anything, so the maximum was approved on child support, pension, and left-over bills. In addition, any hope to reunite and reconcile was gone. My wife wrote me off as a failure.

In March of 2000, I got a call at work from my doctor's nurse. She had known me over the years and for some reason kept my file on her desk since my last visit in January.

She asked me how my new life was going. I replied, "What new life? I am still waiting to die and hoping each day to not wake up."

She replied, "You did not go to rehab? We had it approved in February. In fact, your case was unique because your insurance deemed you a failure at rehab and refused to approve another treatment facility." She went on to explain that my doctor and the counselors and therapist put together a justification for additional treatment and fought hard for me to get help. My insurance bought off on it.

I do not know if I skipped through her voicemail or if I accidently deleted it, but I told her I never got that call. She said she would get right back to me.

About 10 minutes later, she called and said the insurance would still cover but only if I reported to the facility the next day. This meant that I would need to go to my manager and human resources and tell my ex-wife and kids I would be gone for the next 30 days.

The meeting with my manager and human resources went well. They were hoping for a week or two notice but understood and supported me in going. I did not realize it until then that it was my pride blocking me my whole life in hiding my struggles from my employer.

My ex-wife just said, "Great, now you are just going to up and leave us again like you have in the past." In many ways I had to agree with her because I did not have a good history when it came to recovery.

I asked my doctor where I was going, and he said I was going to La Hacienda in Hunt, Texas. I had updated my voicemail and email out of office to say I was out for an undetermined amount of time, went to say goodbye to my kids, and made one last stop to buy beer, cocaine, and weed.

I drank and drugged all the way there and checked in the early morning hours of March 28, 2000. All I could comprehend at that time was I was out of pocket from life. I would be getting good rest in a heated facility and eat well for the next 30 days. In the back of my mind, I feared going back into the real world in a few weeks because I expected the same results that I previously had. But for now, I would not worry about that.

PART THREE

WHAT IT IS LIKE NOW

Chapter Eight

I Came To Believe

All the sudden, nothing in my past was really bothering me, even though I was brought up in total fear of my parents' discipline, hated by God for my sins, verbally and sexually abused, insecure in myself as a person and sexually insecure, screwed around on by the few partners I had, financially broke, homeless, full of guilt and shame, and divorced twice. I was stuck in my own prison. The biggest problem I had and the one that I was convinced would take me out was my addiction to cocaine, alcohol, and all other mind-altering substances. I just knew that if something did not change within the next thirty days I would surely die.

Little did I know that this would be the last day that I used drugs and alcohol, for good! Thus began the steady transformation of a person who in all sorts of bondage, stuck in my own prison, was about to be free to experience a new peace and purpose in life.

I will spend the next few chapters outlining the course of action that changed my life and removed the drink and drug problem.

After spending three days in detox at the treatment center I was released into the general population, where a strict routine from sunup to sundown followed. There would be nonstop classes on the disease concept, meetings in small groups with a licensed chemical dependency counselor, and individual sessions with counselors as well.

It was with these professionals that I never had a reason to lie or hold back on saying anything. I can only say that I had nothing to lose by telling them everything; however, anything I said was still nothing I would tell my family or friends. I just figured I would never see these people again, so I had nothing to lose.

Others in my group held back, and you could notice it. In the end, it turns out that rigorous honesty is a key ingredient to the first step of a 12-step program, and generally until one is honest with themselves, there is little to no success in being able to complete the steps.

So there I was, in complete compliance, on time for morning meds, the classes, and any counselling sessions scheduled that day. Everyone in that center with me was a complete mess as well. We had a lot in common. First with addiction; it seemed that we could not quit on our own, and we had already lost most material things as well as our families and jobs. Some had legal problems with DWI or possession charges. Jail time was about the only thing I was able to avoid; otherwise, I had experienced the same loss as they did.

So it seemed like I was in the right place. The three previous treatment centers were similar, and I compared these places more like an institution for the mentally insane because we were all crazy to let addiction take us to that point.

There is an adage in the rooms of recovery that says the only things that come out of addiction are jails, institution, and death. How true this is, and for me, I got the first two down and was waiting for the third. I recall thinking to myself that although I accepted that I was going to hell for all the wrongs I did, I was certain I was in a living hell on Earth; in a spot where I did not care if I were living or not. In the end, that is where I was.

In the second week in treatment, I had an overwhelming fear, thinking my time there was wrapping up. A great sadness came over me because I still felt the same as when I got there. Nothing really changed even though I paid attention in the classes, did the reading assignments, and participated fully in my counselling sessions.

I talked to the guy who started us off each morning with an hour-long session on the first step. He would beat the same thing into our heads each day, the same lesson from the "doctor's opinion" through page 44 of the "big book."

When I told him I did not feel any different and was worried about being released soon, he said I had not had a first step experience.

I asked, "How do I get that?"

He said to get out of myself; that my truth would need to travel from my head to my heart, and once being honest to my truth, I would surrender and be open to something else. He went on to explain that once a person has a first step experience, he has God's grace and power to complete the rest of the steps, which would free me from the bondage of addiction.

He then suggested I read from the cover to page 44 and underline anything to which I could relate to. He also said he was giving us the problem every morning and to listen and take the information from my head and move it to my heart.

It turns out that the biggest thing blocking me from having a first step experience; me comparing myself to others. You see, there are those who can use drugs and alcohol socially and never have any monetary, legal, family, or job-related consequences. Then there are those who use drugs and alcohol and do have financial, family, job, legal, or even health issues, but they can stop or moderate given sufficient reason. Then there are those who, once they start drinking or drugging, they cannot stop no matter what.

I could accept these three categories but was confident I fell into the category of I could stop or moderate, given sufficient reason.

So I did what was suggested and started to talk to those who worked at the facility about the first step. The first thing I noticed was they, too, were once as hopeless as myself, but they found a new peace and happiness, and their obsession was removed after following a few simple suggestions.

Key areas of the big book that helped me find my truth and experience the first step were small statements throughout the first 44 pages.

In the doctor's opinion, it talks about the fact that addiction is as old as time, and prior to the 1940s, the only option for those with drug or alcohol addiction was death or an insane asylum. But now, thanks to the book Alcoholics Anonymous published in the 1930s, we have a solution to the madness. The doctor's opinion also states that the medical field had to admit that although they were well educated and had the best technology known, nothing seemed to help the alcoholic and addict. Outside the temporary relief of being locked up in a hospital, always they would end up back where they left off in their drink or drug problem.

The doctor's opinion also stated that the effects of alcohol and drugs is likened to an allergy and only occurs in people like me. That once having ingested the alcohol or drugs, something happens that makes me want to keep using, no matter the knowledge I may have of the dangers that would happen if I do. The good doctor says that those who do not get this allergy effect do a little and put it away. Not so with the real addict/alcoholic. He goes on to say that we hopeless types are beyond human aid.

He does close his opinion with the fact that we are able to recover if we have a shift in our thinking, a type of spiritual transformation inwardly that he had only seen happen with those who submitted to the simple requirements outlined in the big book. He also stated that it appears that those who recover can maintain sobriety by giving away what was so freely given to them. So even though one is hopeless and beyond human aid, he can recover by working with someone who have had a spiritual experienced because of the Twelve Steps.

Up to this point, I had always tried to do this deal on my own and failed miserably.

Now I worked with someone who had been there, and we discussed in length my dilemma. He had pointed things out to me about my story and asked me questions that, after answering, my truth was revealed to me.

My first step experience was my understanding that I was different than those who I knew that drank and drugged. After careful review of my experience, I had to admit that although I did know people who got drunk, and may even have had financial, relationship, and possible legal issues, even though in many ways they looked just like me, the significant difference was the fact that they could stop or moderate, given sufficient reason.

I exclaimed to the person helping me that that is where I was. Now that I was in treatment, this was it! I had sufficient reason to stop.

Then he came back at me with this: "Well, you just told me your story, and you said you had been drinking and drugging since you were 11 years old. Now you are 39. You also told me that you were in three previous treatment centers, and this is your fourth. Regarding your relationships, you only had a few girlfriends who screwed around on you, but you have also been divorced two times. The second marriage ended with two innocent children having to leave their father because his addiction was taking the family down financially and their safety was in jeopardy." He reminded me that they left over three years ago.

Then he piled on evidence that he gathered from my story on what exactly happens when I drink and drug. He reminded me to look at the doctor's opinion and other areas of the first 44 pages and see how my experience maps to those of a hopeless addict. He wanted me to see the truth that once I ingest alcohol or drugs, what happens to me physically, mentally, and spiritually does not happen to the social user. Once I use, I cannot stop even though I want to. That reaction only occurs in the real alcoholic and addict.

He then said that I needed to rethink where I am at because it looked like I had sufficient reason to stop or moderate for at least 12 years prior to our meeting, according to my story.

His words hit me like a ton a bricks. I had no choice but to admit to myself that I was a drug addict and alcoholic, and I was beyond human aid. I wanted so bad to cling to the fact that because I was in treatment again, this was my reason to stop.

What suddenly happened was my truth told me that I would never be cured, that I have this disease and I am beyond human aid. My only choice was to do the only thing known to man up to this day, and that was to have a spiritual awakening.

Therefore, my first step in recovery was to honestly admit to myself that I was an addict and alcoholic, that I had lost the power of choice, and that my life had become unmanageable

I cannot say why I went on for 26 years drinking and drugging when it only took a couple of hours of reading, soul searching, honesty, and working with another addict to come to my first step truth. I remember being happy that I finally had my own diagnosis, and I felt at that time that everything would be okay.

CHAPTER NINE

THE DECISION

This chapter will cover the second and third steps in my recovery. In step two, I came to believe that a power greater than myself could return me to sanity.

Having full knowledge of my dreadful condition, "my truth," it was clear to me that I was insane. After all, who in their right mind would repeat time after time the experiment of the first drink or drug, expecting different results? The results were always the same or worse, never better.

In this step, I had to briefly look at my truth, admit I am powerless, and agree that nothing has changed to this point. I am still beyond human aid. The person sitting across from me who had been through the program explained that I simply had to be open to a power greater than myself.

I came into the program of recovery a churched person; in fact, to this point, I still attended the Catholic Church Masses on a weekly basis, I had also attended holy days of obligation and practiced the sacrament of reconciliation. Yet as in years past, I was spiritually bankrupt. I never really felt anything internally when attending church; I just went through the motions.

What I do know, as stated previously in this book, was my core belief: If you sin, you go to hell. Now I had had this belief since I was five years old. The fear of God, the priest, and my parents—anyone with authority—scared the hell out of me.

I never told my parents I thought God already predestined me to hell; I just believed it. I do not know if that is what I was taught, and I do not know why I never heard about God's forgiveness and grace, but that was my core belief and foundation. I had accepted the fact and even though I held on to that all these years, I found in this step of recovery something had to change.

It is best explained that when faced with no other option but to go on to the bitter end as I knew it, which was a drug addicted death or to accept spiritual help, I was left with those two options.

It was suggested that I let go of any conception of God I had, and that I be open to seeking a new experience. I only had two options. Would I consider starting over regardless of my years of engrained beliefs?

I simply had to look at my experience with the God thing. If all I knew was, He was a punishing God, and if all I knew about religion was tradition, I had to ask myself how that was working for me. Obviously, it was not because I was insane, and it certainly had not relieved me of my addiction. I added this bit of truth to my experience, and I was now ready to be open to a new experience.

It was also explained to me that I did not have to throw away my childhood religious beliefs or stop going to church; I was to just not cling to them as I did and allow a new experience to shape my relationship with God.

This seemed like a reasonable concept. My second step in recovery was that I became willing to be willing to believe in a power greater than myself. I must admit that drugs and alcohol were a great persuader, and they had beat me into a state of reasonableness.

By the time I had completed step three, I had come to believe. In step three, the concept shifts from a "power" to God. I used to think that the Twelve Steps tricked us into the God concept, but what else could that needed power be? I will be forever grateful that the second step knows that we come from varying degrees of beliefs, and some of us no belief at all, so it is natural that they talk about a power greater than ourselves.

In step three, that power is God. I simply had to decide to turn my will and my life over to the care of God *as I understood Him.*

The disclaimer I needed to move on was the part *"as I understood Him"* because remember, the God I knew had already sentenced me to hell. But in step two, I put that aside for now.

The person who was collaborating with me in this step pointed out things that I would need to be convinced of, and based on my experience, I would add those to my truth.

It turns out that those affected by drug and alcoholism take everything to the extreme. We are either all the way to the left or all the way to the right, rarely in the middle.

A worthy exercise was for me to look at how I manage just the basic things in life, like submission to authority, finances, and personal relations, on and on.

You see, the normal person will have the same life experiences that I have. At some point in a human being's lifetime, one might experience good and bad times. There may be times of unemployment due to layoffs or termination, poor health that affects your life savings, the loss of a loved one, getting married, and getting divorced. In all these and more, the addict/alcoholic will react in an extreme nature compared to a normal person who will accept and move on. Why we are different was not to be important at this time; it was just necessary for me to see if I indeed did have the traits as outlined in the third step.

I needed to look at myself and how I wanted to the control the outcome of things, whether my intentions were good in nature or bad.

The recovery text tells me I am driven by a hundred forms of fear, self-delusion, self-centeredness, selfishness, and self-pity. We step on the toes of our fellows, and they retaliate. Then we get angry and harbor resentment.

So I was asked if it was possible that I operated in self-will run riot. Looking back on my life since childhood, with the distrust I have in people and my inner commitment to make sure nobody ever harmed me again, I had to answer yes. In fact, that was part of my survival; to put up walls that would protect me from others. I also used drugs and alcohol to soften the blows that life can deal you.

So now having admitted I was powerless and having become willing to be willing to believe in a power greater than myself, I was to decide to turn my will and my life over to the care of God.

That meant that from here after in life, I was to rely on God in all my affairs. He is my Principal, I am His agent; He is my Father, and I am his child. With that foundation, I could pass into a new existence. I needed to also incorporate Him into my work life relying on His abundance and provisions. I was to seek Him in my personal affairs as well. This was the decision I was to make right now.

The first, second, and third steps are all discussion, but the action steps immediately follow. Although this decision to rely on God seemed impossible, faced with my truth as a hopeless addict and alcoholic, I had little choice. My experience to date is that I go in and out of submission to God and operate in my own will. The blessing is today I have a new awareness when I do that, the pain from operating in self-will brings me back to Him.

It was also made clear to me that we are not expected to be perfect. In fact, nobody is perfect. We are simply to make progress. This I could accept.

So after being fully convinced of my first three steps, I was to say a prayer. My only experience with prayer were the traditional Our Fathers, Hail Mary's, and other repetitive prayers recited in the Catholic Church traditions, so I was lost here.

The gentleman reminded me that I had set aside all my previous conceptions I had, that I could use anything I felt helpful. I decided to create a new prayer life for myself. I treated my newfound power, God, as if He were like any other person I might meet on the street. I no longer could think of Him as a punishing God; I now needed Him more than ever. So I started to pray as if He were with me. Praying is a way that was more of a one-on-one conversation. I had found that to be helpful to me and had incorporated that into a daily prayer life going forward.

So I wrote out my third step, and it went something like this:

> God, I have made a mess of my life. If you would have me, please take me. May I look to You for Your will in my life not mine? Please heal me from the bondages in my life, so I can be used by You to accomplish what You need done. Remove my addiction, so others will see you through me. May I do Your will always?

I was now in my third week of treatment in Hunt, Texas, and one morning, I went up to a hill overlooking a valley armed with my third step prayer. I was told it was best to meet God alone and on my own terms for this step.

The sun was just coming up; it was a very cool morning, but there was no wind. Birds started to chirp as the day started, and it was quiet. I found a tree stump at the edge of the hill. Flat ground behind me and a drop off in front.

I stood on that tree stump, closed my eyes, and extended my hands and arms to the sky. I recited by third step prayer to the God of my understanding. As I was doing that, a whirlwind started up from the ground and went completely up my body. It felt like demons were being pulled out of me and a sudden cleansing feeling came upon me. The crazy thing was that there was no wind prior or after that happened. It was then that I felt the Holy Spirit was with me.

At the end of my third step, I had not only come to believe, but I decided to let God direct me going forward.

CHAPTER TEN

THE FEARLESS LOOK INWARD

In the Twelve Step program, each step is immediately followed by another. For me it was like trudging on to finish a race.

It was explained to me that those with addiction needed to seek a spiritual solution with the desperation of a drowning man. How true it is because, in my case, after 26 years of drinking and drugging, my only sober breaths were while I was in a treatment center.

Here I was again in another treatment center. I had 21 days sober, but this time, there was hope that everything would be okay. Having made my start with the twelve steps, digesting a full understanding of my truth and that I was indeed hopeless, it was in these conditions alone I developed the drive I needed to see what experience I could have next.

It amazed me that my past trauma, childhood fears, religious beliefs, and infidelity brought on to me were no longer important, at least for now. My addiction had been my master. I would have to address that first in order to address other issues and hang-ups in my life.

Having diagnosed my situation as hopeless, being willing to be willing to believe that a power greater than myself could restore my sanity and making the decision to turn my life over to the care of God as I understood Him, I was now on step four.

This is the first action step in the program of recovery. Up to this point, there had been a lot of discussion, but from here on out, for the rest of my life, there would need to be action that would allow me to enlarge my spiritual life.

It was explained to me that resentment was the number one offender. That for addicts and alcoholics in my condition, resentment was fatal, based on the experience of those before me.

The process seemed simple, but here it requires rigorous honesty. I was to start by making a list of people, institutions, and belief systems with whom I was angry.

I have seen people get to this point in recovery and stop. Recalling those who have hurt you and having to see your part in it were too painful, or for some of us, we were not convinced of the first three steps and felt we still had power.

For me, I knew I was beyond human aid, and if this were the only thing that worked for those who went before me, then what was I to do? I made the list.

I did find myself overanalyzing the process, probably because I have perfectionist traits. It was put plainly to me that I was not to be concerned about being perfect. In fact, I was to just pray before I start the simple prayer, "God show me the truth," and to do the next instruction in the basic text of recovery.

The gentleman suggested that if I thought of something, no matter how far back and no matter how trivial, I was to write it down. He explained that if it were no longer a resentment, I would not have thought of it.

So that was my start. I prayed, put pen to paper, and made my list. It amazed me that I was angry at someone or something as far back as when I was five years old.

It was quite a list, and after I looked at it, I realized that an extremely high percentage of every person who was close to me in my life was on it. Immediately, I wished I had found the program of recovery 20 years earlier.

But there it was in black and white in front of me. There was nothing more for me to do but to move on to the next instruction.

Referring to the instructions, I was to make four columns on a sheet of paper. The column headings looked something like this.

I Am Resentful At: **The Cause:**   **Affects My:**   **Where Am I to Blame?**

I was to use one sheet of paper for each person, place, or belief system on the list I just completed.

Now, filling in the columns required honesty and a fearless moral search. Again, I was only to put to paper what came to mind. I was not to overanalyze or hold back anything, regardless how foolish or trivial my resentment seemed. Remembering, more would be revealed.

If I were to reap the benefits of the Twelve Step program, I needed to be honest or risk going back out. I already had column one completed. For each item in my inventory, I needed to list the cause or why I was angry. If there was more than one reason the person made me resentful, I needed to list them all. This is where the craziness comes out because I started to see I was angry over the littlest things.

The third column took thought, but after I understood how to identify how I was affected by the cause and kept it limited to that format, it was time to move on.

It turns out that anger and resentment affect humanity in several ways. It is possible that the cause meant that our personal relations with that person, institution, or belief were affected. Or the cause hit us in our pocketbook. Maybe it was our self-esteem, sex relations, or even our pride that was hurt.

The third column was just that. Listing the areas that were hurt by the cause.

Moving on to the fourth column is where a substantial chunk of truth was revealed to me. The process said that yes, those around me were wrong and did cause harm, but for the addict and alcoholic to only see it that far was fatal. We must be rid of anger, or we will drink or drug, and to do those were to die. Based on my truth so far, I had agreed.

This inventory showed me patterns of behavior, self-protection, and injustice, and how I responded to these. One thing for sure: It humbly showed my where I was at fault. Right, wrong, or indifferent were those who may have hurt me, but who else was there? Me! So in many ways, I had a part in what happened.

CHAPTER ELEVEN

TRUSTING AGAIN

It is amazing how putting pen to paper will reveal the truth. Unless you crumble the paper up or burn it, the truth is there, staring you in the face.

It was now time to share this inventory, my truth, my life story, with another person and God. Being totally convinced that if I balk here or leave something out, I set myself up for more drinking and drugging, I prayed and shared everything that came to mind with my sponsor. This took a couple of evenings after work, but what I thought was so petty, juvenile, or immature the things I did out of trying to protect myself, I found him to have time to listen and was amazed in how many of those same things were done by him. We had a common problem and a common solution.

My experience was so profound I felt cleansed from head to toe, and in fact, I felt the obsession to drink or drug was removed. As I write this 22 years later, the thought of having a drink or drug never returned. It was removed in what I can only explain as a supernatural healing; a miracle.

Being convinced that I needed to complete the Twelve Steps, I moved on. This relief or healing could have convinced me to stop the work, but I had to remember my truth—that if I am an alcoholic and drug addict, I am beyond human aid; and completing the Twelve Step program would lead me to a God who would be with me daily if I stayed close to Him.

Sharing everything with someone else and God opened my eyes to my character defects. My sponsor, who gracefully listened to me, provided a list of character defects he noticed, and my next instruction was to go home.

There, I was to sit in quietness and review steps one through five and honestly ask myself if I left anything out. Then I took the list of defects, and with scales now removed from my eyes, I could humbly see and admit that was me. Closing this quiet time required a prayer that God could have all of me, the good and the bad. I was now willing to let Him into more of my life, allowing Him to remove my character defects so I could be useful to Him and others as I go through life.

From here, I needed to pray for willingness to approach those I have hurt and make amends. My list encompassed decades of people, employers, businesses, churches, creditors, and others, and looking at it seemed like a monumental task. I started to think, *Why I should approach them? What happened was decades ago, surely they had forgotten.* Someone told me my thoughts we off-base because if that were true, I would not be harboring the hurts on myself that happened back to my earliest memories.

Chapter Twelve

Forgiveness

This was about cleaning my side of the street and opening a bigger channel to God, so He could run my life and I could step out of the way.

So I started my amends and approached those I hurt with a sincere expression of what I did and asked how I could make things right. Many were glad I could humbly approach them and just wished me well, and a few did not accept the amends. When I got to my creditors being honest that alcohol and drugs were a part of my mismanagement financially, they either totally forgave my debt or worked out a payment plan with me.

Having hurts I have caused others that were decades long, I also had to travel to make amends to employers I stole from, restaurants I walked out on, and stores I stole from. I even had to travel to a church and make amends for stealing from the collection basket when I was an usher. All these amends went well, and each one provided freedom, humility, and peace. Then, of course, there is the government, the IRS. Although there is not much negotiation, they did set up a payment plan that allowed me to get right with them as well.

I even made amends to the deceased. To be free, they deserved to know I am willing to live a different life too. For these, I wrote out my amends, prayed over them, and read them to someone.

One big amend was also to myself. Yes, I needed to forgive myself, and I could see where I even caused hurts to myself through self-destruction, bad decisions, and a fight-or-flight mentality. This one took a while, and at times, guilt, shame, and remorse will rear their ugly heads, but I was determined to be cleansed and transformed from the inside out. This disease is in the mind and body, and I must be free, period!

I finished my amends within few short months; now I was working with a clean slate in life, or as more clarity came and I remembered something else from the past, I would clean that up as well.

I found freedom in the amends process, specifically in forgiveness from others and forgiving myself. I believe inside each person is a desire to see others live in peace.

Now I was to live like others lived, naturally. The issue here was that I had decades of a conditioned state of living and patterns I developed in how I reacted to what I heard, thought, or did. All these patterns, whether real or fancied, dictated how I would react to others or control the outcome of something. Most people just do not react when they are hurt, they brush it off, or forgive.

This is the difference in someone with deep scars and wounds from past trauma, addiction, and control issues vs. the everyday man. Most men will not react with anger or drown their problems with alcohol or find a temporary reprieve with drugs just to "feel better."

My mode of operation is to cop a resentment, make bad financial decisions, be ugly through anger, drive friends and family away from me, and drink and drug. The difference in me and normal people is that I can't drink socially; I do not stop, and once I start with cocaine, I cannot stop. Knowing the damage these cause, the bottom line is, once these are in my system, something happens and triggers a type of reaction that makes me want more no matter how bad I do not want them. My mind loses the power to choose staying clean. Once in this destructive cycle, the results would be devastating. I would lose my family, have personal relations with friends severed, my vehicles would get repossessed, my 401k would be gone again, and I would get evicted. I would be in a vicious cycle, and this would happen over and over again. At the end, I was sleeping on the side of IH 35, just north of Round Rock, Texas.

Having gone as far as I did to experience the healing I had so far, my truth again spoke to me and said, "Do you really want to live like you did, or do you want to live in peace?" Looking at the paragraph above and reliving it in my mind then comparing it to what I had now was a no brainer. I must move on with no expectations of being like others but being myself as God intended me to be. If others can socially drink and even drug with no consequences, my hat is off to them. For me, to drink and drug means to die.

Chapter Thirteen

Staying Fit Spiritually

To do this required me to make right the wrongs I have done as they happen, not letting them build up over weeks, months or even years.

This proved to me to be difficult. I would have seasons where I was good at it, and seasons where I did not do this and would end up having to do a full-blown inventory again or go insane and fall into my old patterns. The easiest way for me to explain it is that pain is a great motivator. Thankfully, the freedom and experiences I had so far overrode the desire for me to live like I used to.

I do not recommend harboring resentment or letting pride get in the way of this; even if others had a part in it, that only makes life a slippery slope and allows evil to rest in you, keeping you from the freedom you were designed to have.

I am so grateful for my experience so far because my awareness level is remarkably high. My spirit convicts me when I am wrong, and my new way of life will not allow me to live in pain. I must clean up my wrongs as I go. There is no other option, so I strive to not let the sun go down without looking at my day, confessing it to another person and God, and making the amends. This process is required and just part of how all of us are designed to live anyway.

Remember, nobody is perfect, and we all fall short in living how God designed us to live, but there is a way out.

Now a little about prayer and meditation. I have to say that this is the foundation of why I am still sober and healing from trauma for 22 years now. My experience in this area is nothing less than profound.

From my earliest memories, I knew of God, and that was through the Catholic upbringing. But for whatever reason, all I heard was if you sin, you go to hell. So as you can imagine, my experiences as a child, the discipline, horrific sexual abuse, fear, and my end decision to medicate my pain with alcohol and drugs becoming a full-blown addict and alcoholic sealed the truth as I knew it. God hated me, and I was going to hell. Even knowing this, I went to church every week and did what Catholics do, always believing I had to earn my way to heaven.

Decades later in this belief, I ended up in my fourth treatment center in Hunt, Texas. That is where I came to believe. What I mean by that is, my truth of what happens when alcohol and drugs enter my body, the rection to my mind is unlike the reaction in others, and when that happens, nothing good comes from that.

Once I understood the disease and saw my truth, I embraced the fact that, in that condition, there was no turning back, and I was beyond human aid. Then I realized if I am beyond the aid of doctors, hospitals, medication, therapists, and on and on, then what can help me?

Simply put, God can help. At that point of reality and clear thinking, I had no choice but to let Him heal me.

My first real prayer was "God Help Me." It was a start, and from that day on, I do my best to spend time in worship to Him, reading scripture and getting quiet to listen for Him. In my day, if I am confused or needing to make a big decision, I try to pause and wait for an intuitive thought or action. I have now developed incorporating prayer into my life whether it works or not. I already knew and lived the results of not praying and believing God hated me, so this area just became something I do and fully believe it is a huge reason as to why I live a reasonably happy and joyous life, and staying spiritually fit is the primary reason I am clean and sober today.

My sobriety, peace, and joy are related to my daily spiritual condition.

I am not getting churchy here, just stating the facts and experiences for myself and millions of others who have gone before me. I am proud and can boldly say that God needs to be the center of my life. How about yours?

I will leave you here with a suggestion to try it. You do not have to go to church or knock on doors and evangelize about the goodness of God. You need to have a personal relationship with God. That is between you and Him long before you can be useful to others and bear fruit.

Chapter Fourteen

Give It Away

The last step in recovery is to make yourself available to those who have a common problem. If you look around, you will see the uniqueness of every individual. It is amazing that God created us differently, and a fallen world has affected us each differently as well. What happens over time, we learn and again pass along to others the victories over our battles, so when they go through them, they have a better chance to succeed and not suffer as we did.

You do not need to have had trauma as a child with wounds and scars from abuse, addiction, broken marriages, financial blunders, or sex issues. There are people who have not experienced these atrocities; however, they pass on things they have learned to help others.

This is a universal concept that is important for those of us who are healing from trauma and addiction. Remember earlier I said that, if indeed, when alcohol and drugs enter my system, something happens in my mind, body, and spirit that does not happen in others. At some point, I lose control again, and the cycle of addiction kicks in. It makes sense that we need to give away what was so freely given to us. Even though a real alcoholic and addict is beyond human aid, it is critical that a recovered alcoholic/addict be there to guide and hold accountable the man who is seeking a spiritual solution by cleaning up his life.

My experience with these steps was nothing short of a miracle. This entire process, which takes up a good portion of this book, only took about six weeks. I was a full-blown dope fiend, beyond any help, with failure after failure to stop or even moderate on my own.

I spent 26 years drinking and drugging with the last 10 years being pure hell on Earth. I spent six weeks seeking a solution to the problem and had a spiritual experience, and the obsession to drink or drug never returned; it was removed. I have now officially entered humanity.

I devoted my time in the evenings and weekends helping others. Even with my obsession removed, my life was still a mess in my personal relations, finances, and everything else. So I did spend a good five years attending meetings, speaking at halfway houses, and taking meetings to hospitals and institutions, shelters, jails, and prisons. There were hundreds who have been touched, and they touched thousands. That is how it works. Not only was I guiding them on what helped me, this act of giving was like an insurance policy for me. I still must live differently daily and not react like I used to. One thing for sure is that giving my experience aways took me out of myself. That is a blessing.

PART FOUR

REDEMPTION AND TRANSFORMATION

CHAPTER FIFTEEN
AUGUST 11, 2005, 6:00 P.M.

I mentioned I have officially entered humanity after completing the Twelve Steps. In many ways, that is so true. After all, my early childhood with the verbal abuse, physical abuse, and rape placed me in a mindset to not trust anyone and manage survival techniques to be safe and feel better. Making the decision at 12 years old that nobody would ever hurt me again also kick started my alcohol and drug use to a point that, years later, when I tried to stop, I realized I could not.

Thankfully, I met my now wife Karen, and while we lived together a couple of years, we were wanting to get married. I was still attending Catholic Church, and she was going to a Bible church. I knew one of us would have to make a change, so we could worship together. Because the Catholic faith was all I knew, I decided to give her church a try.

I attended with her, got involved in the church, and volunteered. I loved the worship music and the sermons made sense to me, so we became members.

I was now over five years clean and sober, but in the back of my mind, I was thinking I would have to be good the rest of my life to even have a chance to go to heaven when I die. Remember, my foundation in religion was you sin; you go to hell.

We had scheduled pre-marital pastoral counselling to prepare for our November 19, 2005, wedding day.

In the very first session, the pastor said he was glad we were making the decision to marry and that he knew Karen because she had been going there but asked me about myself. I was proud to tell him a condensed version of my upbringing, abuse, addiction, and victory over those bondages.

He then asked me if I thought I would go to heaven if I died today.

I answered that if I were able to live long life and stay committed to spending the rest of my life doing good for others and living the best possible life, I may be able to go to heaven at that point. I just spent the first 40 years of my life in sin.

The pastor graciously explained to me that none of us, not even one, could do enough to earn our way to heaven. Nobody was ever without sin except Jesus Himself, and there are millions of good people in the world who fall short into sin and need forgiveness. That is why God sent Jesus to die on the cross, to pay for our sin—past, present, and future

These words did not confuse me or make me skeptical. In fact, I could accept such a path to salvation. I just never heard that before and was still stuck in the belief system I had grown up with.

I was also thinking, *This profession of faith does not let me off the hook either.* I still needed to live the best life possible going forward; I just did not have to tie it to me going to heaven. A huge weight was lifted off my shoulders to realize I could never work my way to heaven.

I asked the pastor what I needed to do. He told me that if I was ready to let God rule my life and if, in my heart, I would trust Him to do that, I only needed to recite a prayer.

Having believed there was a good God for only five years now and experiencing a supernatural healing miracle, this was not a stretch for be to make this profession of faith. I agreed to say the prayer. That moment was August 11, 2005, at 6:00 P.M.

The prayer went something like this:

> *God, I confess to you I am a sinner, and I now believe that you sent Your Son Jesus to live a perfect life but then to be crucified on a cross, die, descend, and that He was risen up to heaven to conquer evil and to cover my sins, past, present, and future. I ask you to come into my heart, and I trust you with my life and want you to be the Lord over me. Thank You for loving me.*

At that moment, I felt renewed, and physically from my toes through my body and out the top of my head, I felt a rush of renewal. I was alive; my eyes were opened, and I was reborn. This is the most unforgettable time in my life, and I will always remember my statement of faith decision. I am so grateful God had the patience to wait for me. I now had a personal relationship with my Creator.

My prayer is that the person who reads this book and has had similar experiences with trauma and addiction takes the suggestion off this chapter and has his or her own August 11, 2005, experience and passes it on to others. God will use everything, the good and the bad, for our good and His glory.

If you have made a sincere salvation decision, I would love to hear from you by way of the publisher. God will do amazing things in and through you.

If you have not made this decision now and fall into some of the belief systems I had, I encourage you to go to a Bible-based church, get involved in community, read the Bible, pray, and ask to be led into the prayer of salvation.

I started a prayer life/routine early in treatment in March of 2000 because I knew then I was beyond human aid. I am now into my twenty-second year of taking time in the morning to get quiet, listen to worship music, and read the bible. That is how God talks to me in His still soft voice. I am not perfect in this routine in any way, but over time, my time with the Lord has grown, and I do believe that my relationship with God, prayer, and my intentional transformation to live in the image and likeness of Christ is the reason I am sober today. I am also so much more aware of myself and how I fall short daily and need His grace and forgiveness. Without God, I am nothing.

Chapter Sixteen

The Transformation

My real transformation started on March 28, 2000, when I entered that last treatment center in Hunt, Texas. A couple of weeks in, I finally connected the dots as to what happened inside my mind and body when alcohol or drugs enter my system. The reaction I have is unlike others who can socially drink or even drug at times.

This realization was clear to me that if, in fact, I have this disease I am beyond human aid.

That truth leaves no wiggle room for a dying man to recover. The only hope to be free and recovered must come from a higher power whom I choose to call God.

Yes, the same God who, for over 39 years, I thought hated me and was going to send me to hell. The same God who I thought created me to be abused and become a drunk and drug addict. The God who hated me.

I had to decide right then. If, in fact, I had the disease and was beyond human aid, where could I turn? Would I give God a chance to heal me through the Twelve Step program and live in and through me going forward. Of course, I would and that is what you read in Chapters Eight through Fourteen. I am so grateful for my experience and new life I have. That mustard seed of faith to see Him work in and through me was a real gift.

By the way just for practical purposes the ideas and principles outlined in a twelve- step program are really universal, meaning that application of belief, trust, self examination, admission of wrongs amends, quiet time with God and encouragement to others can be used with anyone. These ways to live are all through the Bible as well.

Just to clarify things, I know God can do anything. He can heal anyone from anything just by speaking healing onto that person's sickness or save someone from ongoing terrible sin.

My experience is I needed to cooperate, take action, believe, and enjoy life as He designed it for me. Not anyone else. You too should have your own experience as God has designed each of us uniquely and knew before the universe was blown into existence when we would be born, in what family lines, what would happen in our lives, and he knows the day we will leave this Earth. He had designed each of us with purpose, and as I stated before, He uses the good and bad to expand His Kingdom. As insignificant as you may feel you are, He works with what we have, and trust me, He can do a lot with what we have.

So I declare my transformation started over five years before I accepted Christ as my Lord and Savior. One of the biggest battles in my life, addiction, was removed without explanation other than I got honest with myself and followed the 12 steps as thoroughly and honestly as I could. The only explanation was a miracle, supernatural healing that I could only give the credit to God.

With the addiction behind me, I felt like I was a 39-year-old newborn. The only experiences I had in life were short lived victories, success in business, etcetera, but mostly years of numbing the hurt and not wanting to feel. I really had no real-life experiences that were too good. I went through two marriages, lost my kids, created financial decisions that led to multiple bankruptcies, trouble with the IRS, repossessed vehicles, and other things. I left jobs, got jobs, and left again, seeing success, but my demeanor and lack of trust in others caused difficulties everywhere I worked.

So here I was, clean and sober yet a mess, but I had to start somewhere, and that is exactly what I did. It took me a while to make things right, and along the way, I still made mistakes, especially financial mistakes, that hurt my family, but with each mistake, I would gain wisdom. My current mode of operation would lead any man to say, "This guy is messy," but my faith, having a God who loves me, and just not having the fight in me any longer to run my own life all contribute to my ongoing transformation in eternity.

It seems like I have had more difficulties in sobriety and as a recovered alcoholic/addict and Christian than I did when I was drowning my feelings with poison. One thing for sure is that nothing that has happened to me in the last 22 years ever even made me think about drinking or drugging, and the only reason for that is my truth, a loving wife, and my obedience and personal relationship with God. Period!

In 2008, I started to have recalls of the rapes that happened when I was eight years old. At first, I thought I was crazy, but over a couple days, the complete recall happened, and I saw everything. I remembered the priest's name and relived the horrible rape. Although I obviously knew of the rapes when they occurred, I never told anyone, and I believe that decision I made when I was 12 or maybe even before pushed this memory out. It was the only way I could handle it for decades, and I believe the recall happened at a time in my life when I could deal with it without drinking and drugging myself to death or worse harming myself.

The recall ignited PTSD, and to this day, I have a time or two a year where I fall into a PTSD state. I have learned about it and have been in touch with a wonderful Christian trauma counselor since the recall.

Even this recall did not give me any thought of drinking or drugging myself into oblivion. The years since have been hard on my wife and our extended family when I would have fits of rage, leave jobs for no reason, and just make a mess of things.

The one thing that did not change is my prayer life and thirst for God and His scripture. I feel like that was the glue that held things together during this tough time.

A few years later, while traveling on an airplane, I heard the Lord say, author a book; that someone needed to read it. I was given a vision of the book cover, and the title of each chapter. The result is what you read: my experience as I remember it, my battles won and my desire to get this into the hand of the person who needs to read it.

Everything revealed to me in that flight was lodged into my mind, and I did not even need to write anything down.

That weekend, I started writing, and as I come to the ending chapters here, I will have completed my calling on authoring this book. There were no instructions on how to get through editing, find a literary agent, publisher, or how to market this. All I was told was to write it, and I felt an obligation to be obedient to the direction as it was good not evil, and after what I have been through, I am sure there were people still functional but suffering and living an unhealed life like I did.

So, my transformation into the image and likeness of Christ continues and will continue daily until the day I die. That is how it works.

I still make mistakes and juvenile decisions but have accepted that I am a child of God and free of condemnation. When I am wrong, I know it; I pray and become intentional to change, and that is it. I would not trade my life now for anything else. I am truly blessed. I am very aware of what is good and bad, and the Holy Spirit is my guide.

CHAPTER SEVENTEEN

HEALING LOOKING FORWARD, NOT BACKWARD

The human brain is remarkable, and there is no doubt that somewhere up there is a memory of every single word that was heard; everything I saw through my eyesight; and everything that happened. We each have the biggest supercomputer is the world.

My healing started with victory over addiction; I became willing to be willing to believe that God loved me and accepted Christ as my Lord and Savior.

Those reading this book for pleasure will find it hopeful and a happy story.

But those who suffer in addiction and may be broken from distinct types of abuse and trauma, living a dysfunctional life in secret, will certainly relate to this book and may even be motivated to seek healing in a similar way I did.

When I became free, I was like a newborn starting over, and yes, I still had to seek medical attention over the years and change how I thought and acted, and even change the words that rolled off my tongue. The biggest part of my healing continues to be from prayer and my personal relationship with God. But God also gifted others to help, and my treatment for PTSD, now in its fourteenth year, has proven to be so valuable.

You see, only another recovered drug addict can relate to the man or woman who still suffers from the disease. The suffering and behaviors your loved one's see make them unable to wrap their head around why you cannot stop. The reason for that is what happens in our bodies when alcohol and drugs does not happen in the normal person; therefore, they have no experience why we do the things we do to score our next hit.

Addiction is really the solution to the root cause deep inside us. When I started to drink and drug, it was to kill the pain or fill a void. I did not want to feel. For over two decades, I enjoyed it and had few consequences. However, the day I wanted to put it all down, I spent 10 years trying to manage my usage. I failed miserably.

I was always hard on myself: never thought I was good enough; feared what others thought of me; and lived in the past, not the present. Part of my healing was, yes, to acknowledge the past but stop dwelling, blaming, and falling into remorse, guilt, and shame. I obviously needed to make things right with others to hopefully free them from the wounds I caused, but I needed to forgive myself too.

Today, I rarely consume my thought life with memories of the past. That was a real time waster and fueled the chronic depression I had.

In my experience, I had to address the addiction first before looking at the root cause. The root cause was what happened to me as a young defenseless child—things I could never tell anyone about; but from a young age, I made a plan of life that would protect me.

I started collaborating with a counselor who held me accountable. I always felt comfortable talking to someone who did not know me and who could not hurt me.

Looking at the memories and letting them go were beneficial because when something would trigger me into PTSD, it eventually had no power over me.

I encourage everyone to seek help in this area. After all, God gave us all gifts, and there are doctors, LCDCs, psychologists, treatment centers, recovery ministries, support groups, etc., that are gifted in helping.

I needed this type of support in addition to the spiritual solution. It might seem like a lot of work, but honestly, it took less energy to surrender and allow healing over time to happen versus plotting and planning who I was going to manipulate, what I was going to steal and pawn, or what length I would go to so I could score more drugs.

CHAPTER 18

HOPE ON A DAILY BASIS

As we now navigate to the end of this book, I just want to encourage you that if you have any of the symptoms or hidden wounds that you have never dealt with and if the byproduct of those wounds are causing you calamity in your mental health, personal relations, spirit, work life, or you act out sexually or in fits of rage or addictions, there is hope.

The starting point is honesty achieved by looking at your truth. This is usually done with the help or guidance of someone who has been through similar things and has healed, or who is further along in the healing process than you are.

I invite you to consider healing from the past. Use any resource available starting with God because He has a plan for you too, and He can use the good and the bad for your good, His Glory, and someone will benefit in His Kingdom from your testimony.

The starting point of my healing began with my truth that I was beyond human aid. That opened the only possibility for me to consider, and that was healing through God. My first prayer that I really meant and was the starting point of my surrender was, "God Help Me!

God wants a personal relationship with all of us; He is just waiting for you to turn around and seek Him. This in no way must be a ritual or long, drawn-out prayers typically heard in churches. He just wants you to have a conversation with Him as if He were sitting across from you in a chair in your living room. Practice this and be consistent and intentional, and if you really are beyond human aid in your addiction or life in general, you will be amazed by the results.

One final note as your prayer life builds: You will find that you are doing the talking. That is okay because God wants your petitions for blessings in healing, mental health, physical ailments, finances, family, work, etc. One thing He would like is for you to listen as well. Hearing God is done in every way imaginable. You can hear Him in your suffering, in your joy, in times of plenty or times of little. He can be heard in your obedience or disobedience, through other people or through an intuitive thought or action when confused. He can be heard in nature: in the stars on a pitch-black night; a flower sprouting in the crack of a rock; birds chirping on a quiet spring day; the noise of ocean waves crashing on the shoreline. Because He created everything, He can use everything to get our attention, to talk to us to get us thinking for even a moment about what you just saw, heard, or felt.

The best way to hear Him is to read scripture as often as possible. You will be amazed how problems we face individually, as a nation, or throughout the world have been around forever. The consistent theme or solution in the Bible is always pointing to Jesus. Accept the invitation of Salvation and allow the Holy Spirit to be in you while you are still on this Earth. You will not regret this.

I believe in the power of prayer, and for me to grow deeper into the image and likeness of Christ, I am positive that my prayer life and personal relationship with God play a huge role in my healing.

The peace and joy I have experienced through the healing process was so freeing, I cannot even explain. Am I perfect now? In no way! Nobody is. But I am not the man I used to be, or the little boy stuck in his own prison. I am redeemed.

I can look back today without shame, guilt, or remorse and be thankful I have done something with my hurts, hang ups, wounds, and addictions. I hope the same healing peace and joy will fill your heart as well.

Chapter 19

To The Reader

Family Members,

To those who have family members or friends suffering from childhood trauma, drug-induced mental health issues, and addictions, and you have come to the end of your rope to understand or help the person, I am so sorry. It took me years of sobriety before I saw with clarity the hurt I have caused my family from my selfish, self-centered, drug and alcohol addicted way of living.

The disease of addiction and wounds inflicted by abuse, neglect and alike in those suffering is beyond your help. Help must come from a power greater than themselves. Thank you for loving them as much as you did. There is healing needed for yourself as well but never give up on them in your prayer life.

Seek help for yourself as well, and if there are things you may have done when they were children and know now it was wrong, make those amends; break the cycle if you are still in it, and move on. This disease is not like any other. If a person has terminal cancer, the family and friends will stay by their side until they are gone. Not so with alcoholism, drug addiction, or drug-induced mental illness. This disease drives everyone away because you cannot stand seeing what they are going through, and it is too painful for you as well. They seem beyond hope.

Recovery Ministries, Treatment Centers, and Support Groups,

Thank you for all you do in service work and your heart for the hopeless. It was in my fourth treatment center that I was whipped enough to understand that I really had a disease, and I was beyond human aid. Keep pushing the people you meet and let them self-diagnose, as any chance for healing must come from within each person's heart. Just like me, many people will show because they are forced in by their families, wives, employers, or the legal system. And just like me, if they are not ready, they will leave and go right back into the cycle. What usually happens—assuming they live—and if they are the real deal, they will be back and prayerfully something will click, so they too can recover and begin to peel the onion back and heal in the underlying causes of their disease and mental illness.

Medical and Psychological Professionals,

Thank you so much for the attempts to use medical science to assist clients like me. Thankfully, many in your profession will admit that a pill or shot will not remove the obsession within a real alcoholic or addict and that only abstinence will work. The problem is that if the alcoholic and addict has utterly lost the power of choice, he or she will not be able to abstain for any period of time. I appreciate all you have done for me and not giving up on me. If there was no front-line defense for us, we may not ever get directed to treatment centers, support groups, or some type of faith-based ministry.

To the Person This Was Written For,

If you were able to identify with a fraction of the craziness around the wounds and suffering I endured, things like childhood trauma, physical and verbal abuse, sexual abuse, rape, addictions, dysfunctional relationships, jumping from job to job, thoughts of suicide, chronic depression, PTSD, dissociative disorder, operating mentally in compartments, fits of rage and anger, low self-worth, and a sense of giving up on life just to name a few, this book was written specifically for you. My hope is that you will have enough strength and be at a point in your life to find your truth. Then I pray you recover and heal, and then pass your hope, joy, and peace on to someone else. It is what you are going to do with your new life that will be significant and bear fruit for His Kingdom.